With Knife and Fork in Bulgaria

Mags Pie

Published by Mags Pie, 2023.

While every precaution has been taken in the preparation of this book, the publisher assumes no responsibility for errors or omissions, or for damages resulting from the use of the information contained herein.

WITH KNIFE AND FORK IN BULGARIA

First edition. December 19, 2023.

Copyright © 2023 Mags Pie.

ISBN: 979-8223670094

Written by Mags Pie.

Table of Contents

To my ancestors and great-grandparents who
preserved the spirit and flavors of our land.

With Knife and Fork in Bulgaria

Delicious Travel Tips by Mags Pie

Mags Pie

Introduction

Embark on a captivating journey through the heart of Bulgaria with my latest book, "With Knife and Fork in Bulgaria." As your culinary guide and history enthusiast, I will weave a tapestry of fascinating tales, blending the rich history of cities and small towns with the delectable tapestry of Bulgarian cuisine.

Explore hidden gems and iconic landmarks as we uncover the untold stories behind each place. From the cobbled streets of historic cities to the charming essence of quaint villages, every page is a delightful adventure through Bulgaria's cultural tapestry.

But it's not just about the sights; it's a culinary escapade too. Together, we'll savor the unique flavors and aromas that define Bulgarian gastronomy. With a knife and fork in hand, dive into the diverse world of Bulgarian cuisine, from hearty traditional dishes to modern culinary innovations. Each chapter is a celebration of the country's culinary heritage, showcasing the importance of food in shaping Bulgaria's identity.

Whether you're a history buff, a foodie, or simply an adventurer at heart, "With Knife and Fork in Bulgaria" is a literary feast that promises to leave you hungry for more. Mags Pie's signature blend of wit, insight, and mouth-watering descriptions will transport you to the heart of Bulgaria, where every page is a discovery and every meal is a celebration.

The cities in the bosom of the Balkans

Koprivshtitsa, Karlovo, Kalofer, Kazanlak... the names flow into each other like beads of a rosary, imbued with the spirit of the Renaissance heroes, the mighty energy of the Balkans, the fragrance of oil-bearing roses and reflections of the Thracian golden treasures. In these clean, serene and peaceful towns, time flows slowly, immersed in the contemplation of the turbulent past and immersed in the mysteries of existence.

KOPRIVSHTITZA

The origin of the small town in the heart of Sredna Gora is shrouded in romantic legends about descendants of noble families and far-sighted boyars. It is a fact that during the Turkish rule, Koprivshtitsa enjoyed a number of privileges and maintained its prosperity. On the other hand, it attracts the attention of the Kurdzhaliyas - unruly bands of robbers who plunder and burn the city three times. Today, Koprivshtitsa is an archaeological monument under the open sky with winding cobbled streets, the humpback bridge, the church of Saint Nicholas and the church of the Holy Mother of God, which burned down in 1810, with a preserved silver-plated gospel from 1644, high stone walls, heavy wooden gates behind which are hidden revival house-museums in rich colors. Renaissance architecture is one of the peaks of the national Renaissance, which, due to historical vicissitudes and the fate of Bulgaria, appeared much later than the European one - in the middle and end of the 19th century. Many national heroes, poets and revolutionaries were born here (Todor Kableshkov, Georgi Benkovski, Lyuben Karavelov, Dimcho Debelyanov), the April Uprising broke out here on April 20, 1876 and drew the attention of the world public to the struggle for national independence.

In the picturesque guest houses and restaurants, you can try tempting pasta products - toasted purlenki, fluffy Babin tutmanik and Koprivshtensky mill, ovcha sazderma (meat from a local breed of sheep fried in its own fat), as well as traditional kavarma and pitcher kebab - hearty and hearty Balkan dishes.

The cities of roses

Karlovo

"Karlovo is most beautiful in the days of rose picking. The Karlovo field ripples like a sea, the surface of which covers sometimes rose fields, sometimes mint gardens... The air is light and filled with the aroma of various medicinal and field flowers... All over the streets, endless wreaths of roses, hung on pillars, windows, gates and balconies, the homes are decorated as are the churches and squares." (1936 travelogue)

The national hero of Bulgaria, the Apostle of Freedom Vasil Levski, was born here. The history of the city takes us back through the centuries, all the way to the early Middle Ages, when there were churches and monasteries built on the ruins of ancient pagan sanctuaries. In the era of the Renaissance, fine crafts flourished here - cultivation of rose oil and distillation of rose oil, tannery, pipe-making, coppersmithing, coppersmithing, glassmaking, goldsmithing and gunpowder production. A walk in the Old Town under the rum of the fountains immerses you in the atmosphere of over a hundred Renaissance houses, which today are monuments of culture and are open to visitors. The special value of the royal houses lies in the wood carvings on the ceilings, the decorated gates and the wonderful frescoes on the stone walls. In the courtyards, the fragrant shade of the vineyard, flower beds and boxwood awaits you. An interesting place is the Owl Inn, which functions as a Center for Crafts and Cultural Traditions and is one of the most interesting historical buildings in the Old Town. Here you can get acquainted with the talent and skills of local woodcarvers, cutlers, engravers, coppersmiths, coopers, icon painters, admire the beauty of Karlovy lace and see how kuker masks and pipes are made. In the Historical Museum, in addition to various artifacts from different eras, many documents and authentic weapons related to the national liberation movements and the Russo-Turkish War of Liberation (1877-1878) are exhibited.

The local delicacies head several categories – the famous Karlovy Muscat brandy and aniseed brandy, the magnificent dry white wines from red musket grapes (Muscat and Chardonnay, wines with a sparkling yellow-green color and a subtle fruity aroma) and the Karlovian sujuci and lukanki. Let's not forget the souvenirs with the scent of roses - world famous organic cosmetics, Gyul brandy, rose jam and honey, rose, mint and lavender essential oil.

The Rose Festival is one of the most remarkable festivals in Bulgaria, which

was celebrated for the first time in 1888 in Pavel Banya, and since 1903 in Kazanlak, and since then it has traditionally been held on the first Saturday of June or the last Saturday of May. This is the period when the oil-bearing Kazanlak rose blooms and fills the air with its fragrance. Today, the Rose Festival has become an international celebration that entertains thousands of tourists and guests of the area. Here, in the open air, craftsmen and artists present their works and applied creativity. The culmination of the Festival is on the last day, when the Rosober and Rosovarene rituals are performed using traditional and modern methods, after which a spectacular procession passes through the streets of the city (Karlovo or Kazanlak, on a rotating basis). A volley of cherry balls heralds the end of the celebration.

Kazanlak

Located in the geographical center of the country, in the heart of the Valley of Thracian rulers and roses, Kazanlak is famous as a city of artists and wealthy merchants. Recently discovered gold, silver and bronze finds from Thracian tombs in the region are exhibited in the vault hall of the Historical Museum, the most famous of which are Golyama Kosmatka and Svetitsa and the finds from the ancient city of Sevtopolis. A pleasant walk in Tulbeto Park leads to the Kazanlak Tomb, which dates from the 3rd - 4th centuries BC. and was accidentally discovered in 1944 by soldiers who were digging a trench in the northeastern part of Kazanlak and included in the UNESCO World Heritage List in 1979. The magnificent frescoes in the corridor and the dome room are some of the best preserved works of antiquity painting and can be seen in the copy of the tomb, which is open to visitors. Today, the site is part of the Valley of the Thracian Kings, which also includes the temples and tombs discovered in the last decade (Golyama Kosmatka, Shushmanets, Helvetia, Griffoni, Svetitsa and Ostrusha) and attracting lovers of archeology and virtual travel in antiquity. Among the most impressive artefacts is the image of a beautiful female head, preserved in one of the cassettes forming the structure of the burial chamber in the tomb-cult complex Ostrusha and the widely known golden mask, as well as a bronze head, allegedly of King Sevtus III, ruler of Seutopolis, discovered in Goliamata kosmatka, one of the most magnificent Thracian tombs on the Bulgarian lands.

Kazanlak is known throughout Bulgaria for its legendary donuts, katmi and milinka - pasta products capable of ruining any diet, and jams of green walnuts with endrishe, cherry jam, forgotten delicacies rachel (transparent, golden pieces of pumpkin in aromatic sugar syrup, which are crispy on the outside and soft and juicy on the inside) and petmez (thick grape, watermelon or sugar beet syrup, with the consistency of liquid honey) and the traditional rose jam, of course. The real temptations come from the nearby villages of Maglizh and Enina, and from crystal clear lakes - thick sheep's yogurt, snow-white cheese, sun-ripened and river-watered garden vegetables, forest mushrooms and freshwater fish, ecologically clean products prepared according to traditional recipes and charged with the ringing energy of the Balkans.

In the footsteps of heroes

12 km from Kazanlak, in the foothills of Stara Planina above the town of Shipka, rises the beautiful Shipchen Monastery of the Nativity of Christ, built in honor of the fallen Russian soldiers and Bulgarian militiamen in the Russo-Turkish War of Independence (1877-1878). The monastery complex consists of a Russian-style church and gilded domes that keep the bones of dozens of Russian soldiers who died in the battles for the summit, a monastic building, a pilgrim building, a shelter and a seminary built under the guidance of Russian architects. The funds for its construction were collected through donations collected mainly in Russia. The initiative for its construction was taken by Count Ignatiev and Olga Skobeleva, mother of Russian Major General Mikhail Skobelev. The seventeen huge bells, the largest of which weighs 12 tons, were cast from 30 tons of fired cannon shells, collected in the battle area. 28 km from Kazanlak, on top of Shipka (1326 m) and to the east of the Shipchen Pass, is the open- air museum of the same name. In 1934, the Freedom Monument was built on top, which is reached by a road and 890 stone steps. The huge monument is open for visits with a museum exposition on five floors, and from the top there is a wonderful panoramic view of Gabrovo and Kazanlak.

The Russian-Turkish War of 1877-1878 was fought between Russia and the Ottoman Empire. The war ends with the victory of Russia and the conclusion of the San Stefano Peace Treaty. It brings full independence to Serbia, Romania and Montenegro, and part of Bulgaria is declared a vassal principality. The other part of Bulgaria remained within the borders of the empire as the autonomous region of Eastern Rumelia, which in the fall of 1885 was united with the Principality of Bulgaria.

The old capital cities of Bulgaria

HISTORY IS MOST FASCINATING when you immerse yourself in it and transport yourself to the scene of events that set its direction. A walk in the ancient capitals of Bulgaria will saturate your senses with exciting images and sensations, carved in stone legends of brave rulers and dedicated hermits, striking buildings, captivating murals and elaborate crafts.

Only 70 km from Varna are three archaeological treasures - the two medieval Bulgarian capitals of Pliska and Veliki Preslav, and the Madar Horseman - which will leave a deep impression on your mind.

This is how the Tarnovo inscription, carved in a column kept in the church Holy Forty Martyrs in Veliko Tarnovo, conveys to us the testament of Khan Omurtag:

"A person, even if he lives well, dies and another is born. Let the one born later, looking at this inscription, remember the one who made it. And the archon's name is Khan Omortag Yuvigi. May God honor him to live a hundred years."

Byala Pliska (capital from 681 to 893)

The first capital dates back to the founding of the Bulgarian state in the summer of 681, when the Byzantine emperor Constantine IV Pogonat was forced to conclude a peace treaty with Khan Asparukh and to recognize the new state diplomatically and legally.

The name Pliska means sunny or shining city, probably because of the white marble from which the stately buildings were built. Conceived and built with a strategic plan and an impressive scale, Pliska became one of the most well-developed and beautiful cities of Early Medieval Europe. Located at a crossroads, without relying on natural defense structures, but surrounded by a powerful fortress wall, Pliska seems to issue a silent challenge. Conceived in the form of three concentric circles, the city was surrounded by a rampart and an earthen moat filled with water, 7-9 meters deep and 10 meters wide. Small craftsmen and farmers lived in the first, outer circle of the city. The inner city was inhabited by boyars and nobles, providing all comforts and security thanks to the Citadel, whose walls are over 2 meters thick and equipped with imposing gates.

The capital was built in three stages, with the most significant contribution of three rulers: Khan Krum, Khan Omurtag and Tsar Boris I.

Khan Krum's palace was built on an area of 500 square meters, on two floors and equipped with bathrooms, its own reservoir and a system of secret entrances. Khan Omurtag built the mighty fortress walls and the small palace in the heart of the innermost city, exciting the imagination with an ornate Throne Hall, a water system that has been preserved to this day, a heating system and two temples. The most notable monument from the third stage is the Great Basilica, completed in 875 and now restored and open to visitors. It is a complex including a temple, an archbishop's palace and a monastery built by Tsar Boris I, the ruler who imposed Christianity and introduced the Slavic script to Bulgaria. For 250 years, the Basilica performed the functions of a cathedral and a princely, episcopal and monastery church, the center of spiritual and religious life in early-medieval Bulgaria. In 866, it welcomed the students of Cyril and Methodius, who laid the foundations of the first Slavic literary school. The magnificent temple impresses with its size (100 by 30 meters) and the rich decoration of mosaics and marble columns. Thanks to the restoration works, today you can walk around the complex and capture the atmosphere of the era, walking along the paved road built more than a millennium ago, along which the royal processions once passed.

Near the archaeological complex is the "Cyrillic Court", where one finds himself in the world of books spiritually and physically to experience a unique synesthesia. In the Yard of Letters, hand-carved sculptures of letters and various Slavic symbols await you, along with the figures of their creators - the holy brothers Cyril and Methodius and the tsar Saint Boris I Michael, the Baptist. Next to a small chapel stands a traditional Armenian khachkar (stone with a cross), a gift from the Armenian people. Two halls in the stone fortress with towers and battlements tell the story of the Cyrillic alphabet in Bulgaria, and the Alley of Writers presents authors from different cultures who wrote in Cyrillic.

Veliki Preslav

After a turn on the narrow road, Preslav appeared. Buildings and fortress walls, golden domes and high roofs merged into one — and the city, folded on scattered hills, overhung the river Tucha, which right here escaped from a gorge and formed the beautiful Estuary.

(The quote is from the book Tsar Simeon by Dimitar Mantov, 1979)

Preslav was founded by Khan Omurtag, but began its path to a great and glorious city in the fateful year 893. Strategically located, gathering the rays of the most important roads of the state and foreign merchants, protected from all sides, equipped with three great passes and never-ending waters on the Kamchia River, the city carries out its spiritual and educational mission in the history of Bulgaria.

And so, in 893, the Council of Preslav was held, proclaiming Christianity as the official religion, the Old Bulgarian language as the official language of the young state, and the independence of the Bulgarian church from the Byzantine one. King Simeon the Great ascended the throne and moved the capital from Pliska to Preslav.

The city was designed on a grand scale, spread over an area of 3.5 square meters, surrounded by two concentric fortress walls of white stone, with towers, four gates and a magnificent palace equipped with sewers and water supply. The palaces are built of marble and the mortar has a slightly pink tint. The round windows were glazed with blue and green panels. Perhaps the most remarkable is the Round Church, called Golden because of its gilded dome, which evokes associations with the culture of Central Asia. The church is erected on a hill outside the city walls, far from the worldly bustle, beautiful and noble in its solitude.

The city became a center of literature and books in 893, when King Simeon I moved here the Preslav School of Literature founded in Pliska, which became the most important center for literature, translation, painting and ceramics. The oldest Cyrillic texts were also found here.

In the Archaeological Museum in Preslav you can see part of a magnificent gold treasure consisting of 120 amazingly beautiful ornaments, some made in the 10th century and others earlier, probably belonging to a medieval princess.

Madara Horseman

What a challenge to the senses and the imagination is this medieval bas-relief that emerges and gradually takes shape in the distance! Whose masterly hands carved this mighty horseman in lifelike proportions on the high sheer rock... The symbolism of the images - a horseman, a dog, a lion and an eagle - evokes associations with the eternal archetype of the warrior who has mastered his thought, power and ambition. The first surveys of the area began in 1892, and in 1979 the Madar horseman was declared by UNESCO a monument of world and cultural heritage and recognized as the only rock relief in Europe from the era of the Early Middle Ages. Hungarian traveler Felix Kanitz was intrigued by the figure and suggested that it dates back to the Roman Empire. Historians and researchers propose different hypotheses for the prototype of the Horseman - from a Thracian king to a proto-Bulgarian hero or a collective image of the early khans and kings of the Bulgarian state.

Veliko Tarnovo

One of the most romantic and picturesque cities of Bulgaria with a thousand-year history, Veliko Tarnovo radiates dignity, nobility and charm. The city was proclaimed the capital of the Second Bulgarian Kingdom in 1185, when the brothers Ivan-Asen and Teodor-Peter rejected Byzantine rule and declared independence.

The city amazes with its location and architecture. Located on four hills - Tsarevets, Trapezitsa, Sveta Gora and Momina Fortress - and arranged amphitheatrically, Tarnovo or Tarnovgrad knows the recipe for love at first sight - sloping cobblestone streets, the full-water Yantra, the characteristic technique of mixed construction of different types of stone and bricks arranged to form decorative ornaments and monograms, boyar houses with filigree ceramic decoration, fairy palaces and ancient legends. The palace complex, the Patriarchate, Tsarevets, the Baldwin Tower and the evening show under the open sky Sound and Light presenting the history of the Second Bulgarian Kingdom, the Church of Saint Demetrius of Thessaloniki, as well as the boyar settlement of Arbanasi are only the biggest pearls in the crown of the old capital city.

A story of love and betrayal

Legend has it that in battle King Kaloyan captured the Latin emperor Baldwin of Flanders and imprisoned him in one of the towers of Tsarevets. The king's wife, the Cuman princess Anna-Anisia, fell in love with the captive and secretly sent him a letter in which she suggested that they escape together. However, the emperor did not give in and created in her heart an insult and a thirst for revenge. Therefore, the queen accused the knight of trying to seduce her, and he was punished with death.

The Black Sea pearls To Bulgaria

Nessebar, Pomorie, Chernomorets, Sozopol, Primorsko, Kiten, Tsarevo and Ahtopol... magical places strung together like pearls from a child's necklace - authentic and different, unpretentious and bewitchingly beautiful, they look around the waters of the Black Sea and cast reflections on the mother-of-pearl interior of the black clams. In their names are woven legends of ancient seafarers and seekers of happiness, archeology constantly surprises us with discoveries that tickle the imagination. Here, the flavors of the dishes are a legacy of the ancient Black Sea cultures, and the intoxicating scents of green fig jam, lace sweets and bursting ripe pomegranates envelop you like a seductive incense.

This modest topographical map of the treasures along the Bulgarian Black Sea coast is only a guide, aiming to set a direction and whet your appetite for the discoveries you are about to make. Coastal cities offer the perfect balance between past and present: the remarkable heritage of Thracian, Byzantine, Roman and Bulgarian culture and the folklore traditions of the local population. Thanks to their location, at the crossroads of sea routes in the Black Sea and the Balkans, these settlements have been of strategic importance for millennia. And although we do not pay special attention to the big cities like Varna, we cannot fail to mention that the sea capital guards the oldest gold treasure in the world - a fact that is unknown to most tourists. It was discovered in the Varna Chalcolithic necropolis, which dates back to around 4400 BC. The city has the only dolphinarium, an astrological observatory and a planetarium, as well as an aquarium, which are located in the Sea Garden, the second largest park in Bulgaria.

Nessebar

Perched on a romantic cliff peninsula, it is one of the most ancient cities in Europe, founded more than 3200 years ago by the Thracians, who called it Melsambria. In the 6th century BC, the city attracted the attention of Greek settlers, and later the Romans, Slavs and Bulgarians. The name gradually transformed into Mesemvria and Nessebar. The old town is included in the UNESCO World Heritage List (1983). Hidden behind massive fortress walls from the time of the Thracians and Dorians, standing out dramatically against the background of the rocky coast, the azure sky and the deep blue of the sea, Nessebar is a treasure trove of secrets, legends and artifacts.

A walk through the narrow cobbled streets with the typical Black Sea houses, the amphitheater, the Byzantine baths, ruins and ancient churches is like traveling in a time machine - the basilica museum of Saint Stephen (XI-XIII century, painted in 1599), the unfinished church of Saint John Aliturgetus (14th century), the preserved medieval church of Christ Pantocrator (13th - 14th centuries), the church-museum of Saint Spas (1609), the churches of Saint Paraskeva and Saint Sophia, the churches of Saint John the Baptist and Saint Michael and Gabriel, the remains of the Basilica of the Virgin Eleusis... The windmills - one at the beginning and the other in the middle of the isthmus connecting the Old and the New Town - are one of the symbols of Nessebar.

In the evening, the Old Town turns into a dramatic setting for a lazy stroll in search of impressive views, unexpected finds in the souvenir shops, lace masterpieces that came out from under the gnarled fingers of the squatters in front of the grandmother's houses, and culinary revelations. Whether you choose a concert under the stars in the Ancient Theater, gazing at the sea from an elegant beach bar or tasting the dishes in a small family restaurant, Nessebar will win your heart and palate. Local specialties revolve around the fishermen's catch - fish soup, fried turbot with garlic skordalia sauce, smoked bonito, veyan karagioz, lefer on tile. Archaeologists recently discovered 30 amphorae, part of an ancient wine cellar more than 2,500 years old, so be sure to enjoy a glass of cold white wine under the intoxicating shade of the fig trees.

Pomorie

The Black Pearl is located on a small rocky peninsula between Burgas and Sunny Beach and beckons with red-hot black sand beaches and clear, warm sea. In the morning before sunrise, the air vibrates with energy, charged with ozone and negative ions, ultraviolet rays and iodine vapors from seaweed. There is no better place for a combined spa therapy – the sea, the warm mineral springs and the healing mud and lye from Lake Pomorie seem to be competing to bestow their healing and restorative properties. The "white and black gold" of Pomorie are the salt, which has been mined here for 2,500 years using authentic technology, and the estuary mud from the bottom of Lake Pomorie. It is no coincidence that in ancient times the Anchial nymphs, protectors of the springs, were worshiped here. Among the sights of Anchialo, as is the old name of the city, are the men's monastery of Saint George the Victorious, the Church of the Holy Transfiguration of the Lord, the Pomorie dome tomb (hiron) and the Old Pomorie houses.

In Pomorie, you can enjoy products from the nearby organic dairies, try bulgur and nettle pie and eat real baklava and kadaif while sipping coffee brewed on the grill. The trademark of the region is the wines, brandy and brandy from the famous Pomorie cellars. Here is the largest cellar on the

Balkan Peninsula, built in 1932 in a beautiful park by the sea. You can taste the grape elixir at different stages of ripening and learn about the intricacies of winemaking.

Chernomorets

Tucked away in a small horseshoe-shaped bay, which the Greeks called Agios Nikolaos (St. Nicholas), Chernomorets shyly opens before your eyes a magnificent view of Cape Emine to the north and Arcutino to the south, as if embarrassed by the exquisite beauty of Sozopol, from which it is only separated 9 kilometers. The picturesque nature and warm waters of the bay create a feeling of a garden of paradise. Five idyllic beaches await you - sometimes quiet and sandy with clean, shallow waters, sometimes wild and rocky, ideal for diving and spearfishing, sometimes gorgeous on the Tsar's beach at the Gradina campsite. In the heart of the town you will find the Church of Saint Nicholas and the Garden of Eden.

The main merit of the local cuisine is that it relies on regional eco products, grown and prepared by the caring hands of the local housewives according to strictly guarded family recipes. Enjoy a seafood pub or a trap under the asma and embark on a culinary journey - tarator, thumb-sized grape sarmi, wrapped in leaves from the vine above you, grilled saffron, mussels with rice... And to drink, choose the Black Sea classic - ice-cold milky white mastic (a strong anise-flavored alcoholic drink from the family of ouzo, pernot and pastis) or cloud if you like adventure – behind the ambiguous name is a cult marine "cocktail" of mastic and mint or a watermelon cocktail for the ladies.

Since we mentioned the rocky promontory Emine, the easternmost point of the Staroplaninska chain, which divides the Bulgarian Black Sea coast into northern and southern, let's tell the legend about it. According to some sources, the name comes from the Greek name for a stormy, windy place, according to others it is named after the mother of the Prophet Muhammad, but the local people tell a different story. Once the lighthouse keeper was an old sailor who had a wonderfully beautiful daughter. The girl grew up willing and brave. After a sea storm, she saw a shipwreck floating on the waves, threw herself into the waters and saved him. The sailor fell in love with the girl and she returned his feelings. Then he left, but at parting he promised to return to her. Whether he forgot about the given word or trouble befell him - no one knows. But the girl waited for him from sunrise to sunset, standing on the bow. Finally, maddened with despair, she threw herself into the sea and the waves turned crimson. Even today, when the sun rises, the water around the nose turns red and reminds of the dangerous madness of love.

Sozopol

The artistic charm of Sozopol has excited people for millennia. Undoubtedly, the city of Apollo is the most beautiful pearl in the string of Black Sea cities, and the World Tourism and Travel Council chose Sozopol as the second best destination in the world for 2015. Founded in 610 BC by settlers from Asia Minor, the city-state of Apollonia quickly became a thriving trading center hidden behind massive fortress walls and protected by the colossal statue of Apollo the Healer. In 72 BC, the Roman legions captured, burned and sacked Apollonia, taking the statue of its patron to Rome. Restored in the first century, the city became known as Sozopolis, City of Salvation, during the Ottoman period it was called Sizebolu, and after the Liberation it took the name Sozopol.

The city is divided into two parts - old, which is a monument under the auspices of UNESCO, and new, united by the Sea Garden. The old town is a treasure trove of artifacts - a perfectly preserved and restored fortress wall, the relics of St. John the Baptist, discovered in 2010 on the island of St. Ivan and displayed in the church of St. St. Cyril and Methodius, the 7-8 thousand-year-old one-timbered boat exhibited in the Museum testifies to the skills of the ancient seafarers. Another famous exhibit is the ancient vampire displayed behind a glass case, with a face reconstructed from the shape of his skull.

A walk along the cobbled streets of the Old Town or on a yacht by the coast gives you the opportunity to enjoy the aristocratic atmosphere, the noble bearing of the old houses with verandas, the fig trees, the crocheted curtains, the spirit of timelessness and the picturesque views. A trip to the islands of Sozopol is an unforgettable experience. The largest, Saint Ivan, preserves the remains of an ancient monastery, a Thracian sanctuary and an ancient temple complex, above which stands the statue of the healing god Apollo. Next to it is the smaller island of Saint Peter. Over 70 species of birds, many of which are listed in the Red Book of protected species, inhabit the islands and take the thread of Via every year Pontica. South of Sozopol, high rocky shores and exciting caves, carved by the soft chisel of the waves, await you. For diving enthusiasts, there are fantastic underwater sights and even traces of an ancient pirate hideout. Not far away is the Ropotamo Reserve, covering the mouth of the river of the same name. There are boat trips on the river and observation of interesting species of birds and plants.

Castrum Fortress Domini at Cape Skamni is another imaginative landmark, once home to the dreaded pirate Krivich, mentioned in 13th-century Venetian books that describe pirate raids in the Black Sea on their merchant galleys.

Along with legends of pirates and vampires, Sozopol keeps a whole bunch of recipes for tempting dishes. Most of the houses in the old town house charming establishments, each with a unique menu. The local fishermen are second to none, and the fish restaurants along the two coastal streets offer incredible delicacies. Try fish soup according to an authentic recipe, eat chiroz (shade-dried fish, ideal appetizer for ice beer), fried poppets, safrid or chernokop. Old fishermen claim that when the first cosmonaut Yuri Gagarin visited the city more than half a century ago, he was so impressed by the chiros that he bought several bundles of dried fish to take home on his way out.

For dessert, get homemade ice cream made from milk, eggs, cinnamon and caramelized nuts, topped with green fig jam. Another unique specialty that you won't find anywhere else is the dagma – an airy and crunchy lace pastry, generously sprinkled with powdered sugar. Local culinary priestesses say that the technology of the pastry was secretly exported from the Byzantine imperial court and brought here to mark every major holiday. The recipe is a secret and passed down from mother to daughter, the cake is made with a special mold similar to a wheel with twelve spokes, which is kept and passed down in the family. The name of the cake is of Turkish origin and means seal, trace.

Two cult events are held in Sozopol: Sozopol Fest July morning (the night before the first of July) and the Apollonia Arts Festival (September 1-10), which has been held since 1984 until today. These are ten days filled with theater performances, chamber and jazz concerts under the open sky, film screenings, exhibitions and literary evenings, as well as master classes in various specialties - singing, piano, jazz improvisations, theater schools.

According to one legend, the Greek supreme god Zeus had a relationship with a mortal woman, from whom three beautiful daughters were born to him - Siza, Agatha and Visa. One day

Zeus got angry with his daughters and banished them from the sacred Mount Olympus. The three sisters separated and each of them founded a settlement: Siza founded Sozopol, Agatha founded Agatopol (Ahtopol), and Visa founded Urdoviza (Kiten).

Primorsko and Kiten

Beautiful sandy beaches and rounded dunes, Mediterranean climate, beautiful parks, oak forest, citrus fruits, a lively wave of youthful energy and endless celebration. The four beaches of Primorsko offer opportunities for volleyball, water skiing, surfing and children's entertainment. A favorite place of young people since the 1980s, Primorsko is a city with a thousand-year history, surrounded by ruins of ancient settlements, fortress walls, dolmens and necropolises, the Thracian megalithic sanctuary on Cape Begliktash, built in honor of the sun god and dated to the 14th century BC.

We continue to the south and almost imperceptibly enter Kiten, where the forested slopes of Strandzha Mountain are reflected in the azure waters of the sea, and the spacious beaches in the two bays of Karaagach and Atliman beguile with fine golden sand and a variety of attractions. For lovers of water sports, the Balkanika marine base offers equipment and gear for sailing, underwater fishing, underwater archaeology, water skiing and yachts. You can take a pleasant walk in the Ropotamo and Arcutino reserves, where you will enjoy pure nature and rare plants.

Tsarevo and Ahtopol

The further south you go, the nicer and more unpretentiously charming the seaside villages become. The immediate vicinity of Strandzha promises clean food and opportunities for eco- tourism.

Tsarevo, called Vasilikos in the past and Michurin in the period 1950-1991, is a typical fishing town with a developed port and known traditions in shipbuilding, which maintained good trade relations with the capital of the Ottoman Empire and with the ports in the Aegean and Marmara seas. 7 km from the city is the resort village of Lozenets with beautiful wild beaches.

Located on a rocky peninsula, sunny Ahtopol was so beloved by the goddess Agatha that she chose it as her abode and gave it her name - city of love. Here, time moves slowly, the sea breeze caresses like a caress, and the waters are warm and flattering, awakening the spirit of the adventurer. "Every tourist becomes a poet here," the locals joke. Nearby is the village of Kosti, where a fair is held every summer. Nestinar dances, characteristic of the village, preserved from ancient times, are played on it. Traps and small family restaurants stock up on local produce, so you can eat a shop salad of garden tomatoes, cucumbers and peppers and enjoy the taste of the fish from the morning catch, breaded mussels and crappies.

And the smiling hosts will welcome you like old friends and tell you legends of hidden treasures and stories of sea elements that you will never forget.

Veleka River Estuary

The estuary of Veleka River is one of the most picturesque and astonishingly beautiful corners of the Bulgarian Black Sea. There are protected and rare plants, such as the yellow water lily, which can only be found on the territory of the nature park. And the beach at the mouth of the river is among the most preserved and sheltered places on the Black Sea coast.

Aleppo

Aleppo is the name of one of the most beautiful beaches in the south. Translated from Greek, it means fox. From there comes the name of Lisiche blato, which is 6.5 km from Sozopol. By origin, Aleppo is a port. It is separated from the sea by a strip of sand dunes, which are a protected area. The place teems with numerous protected species of waterfowl. Favorite place for nudists, people with dogs, unwanted on crowded beaches.

Arcutino

Arcutino is a beach near the mouth of the Ropotamo River. It is located about 8-10 km from Sozopol. Opposite Arcutino is the Bear Swamp, which is part of the Ropotamo Reserve. The marsh is separated by sand dunes, and a sand lily grows on the beach itself.

From the bay there is a wonderful view of the island of St. Thomas - the only place in Bulgaria where cacti grow wild. The people who visit it are mainly nudists.

Arapya

Between the resorts of Lozenets and Tsarevo is Arapya beach. In the past it was better known as a campsite, but today its territory is dotted with hotels and private houses. Arapia is located in a picturesque bay surrounded by pine and deciduous forests. Ever since the time of socialism, until today it is a favorite place for Polish, Czech and Bulgarian tourists. Favorite surf spot.

Dardanelles

The Dardanelles near the village of Varvara is the name of rocks that are a favorite place for divers. Although there is only one sandy strip and it is very small, it is one of the most beautiful on our Black Sea coast. The village is surrounded by rocky bays suitable for spearfishing and diving. The other amenity of Varvara is the mountain. The merging of Strandzha Mountain with the Black Sea makes Varvara a unique place for Bulgaria.

There are traces of a late antique and medieval fortress on Mount Papia, close to the village.

Sinemorets

The beach of Sinemorets is a place where the river Veleka makes its way through the beach and paints an unforgettable sight. If you go along the rocks to the southeast, you will reach the Korabite area. According to legend, old unnecessary ships were broken up here. A little further is Butamiata - the central and only guarded beach in Sinemorets, which is quite lively.

However, lovers of wild nature can visit one of the few remaining virgin beaches in Bulgaria - Lipite. It is surrounded by forest and is rarely visited. The road there is also suitable for inexperienced tourists and children.

The third beach - Listite can be reached by a goat path and only on foot. Deer and roe deer can be found in these places in the summer.

Silistar

From Ahtopol to Bulgaria's southern border of Rezovo, there are several bays with gorgeous beaches, one of which is Silistar. It is located in the border area with Turkey near Sinemorets. It falls within the territory of the Strandja nature park. Part of the European ecological network Natura 2000. It is untouched by the concrete hysteria along the Black Sea.

Rezovo

Rezovo is a pristine beach right on our border with Turkey. It is said to be a place where time has stood still. What makes Rezovo unique is the limited construction and the presence of nature. Here the evenings are quiet and peaceful, without crowds on the streets. During the day it is visited by many people who come here to see the southernmost point to which Bulgaria extends.

Irakli

I rakli - one of the last 9 natural territories along our Black Sea, unaffected by development. The entire area of Irakli - Emine is in the "Natura 2000" zone.

In the resort of Irakli is one of the most beautiful beaches on our southern Black Sea coast. The beach strip with a length of 3 km is divided by the Vaya River, which flows into the sea forming a wide estuary. As a result, two beaches are formed - Irakli beach north of the river and "Vaya" beach located south in the direction of Cape Emine. The beaches are wide, clean and with pristine white sand.

The central beach of Irakli has a cafe and a small restaurant, with showers and drinking water, with toilets, changing cabins and umbrellas, lifeguards, a doctor and all the necessary conditions for a peaceful holiday.

Shkorpilovtsi

Shkorpilovtsi is one of our largest beaches in the north. It is located between Nessebar and Varna. It continues to be a place of solitude, but according to NIM chief Bozhidar Dimitrov, its future looks Russian. The Moscow City Hall has purchased huge plots of land, which it plans to develop with hotels for Muscovites.

The holiday in Shkorpilovtsi is the lowest possible budget of the entire Black Sea coast, say the initiated. There are restaurants, bars, summer cinema, surf and kite school. The nature around the resort is characterized by its unique diversity and remoteness from other resorts and settlements. The beach is the largest in Bulgaria - 12 km. The vastness of the beach ensures plenty of unoccupied space, even in the peak of the season. The coastline is straight, without a bay, which is also a prerequisite for waves in north and northeast winds. The place is one of the best for practicing surfing, windsurfing and kitesurfing on our Black Sea coast. Here is also the Kamchiski sands reserve.

Cocoa Beach

Cocoa Beach on Sunny Beach is probably the most discussed beach in the forums. Here is the kingdom of biceps and silicone, where you can see sweet Barbies next to expensive cars and young, strong men with shaved heads fussing around them. It is located on the beach in Sunny Beach and has probably existed for about 8-9 years. There are canopied tents with wide white mattresses, from which you can watch the tanned bodies of the beachgoers swaying in the heat.

A place for parties because there are three discos - one for retro music and two with chalga. "It's nice to be in the water to the sound of music and forget all the dirt you saw in Sunny Beach during the day," someone wrote.

Oasis

The beach of the Oasis complex near the village of Lozenets is one of the most modern on our southern Black Sea coast in recent times. A huge hotel surrounds the beach, perfectly maintained beach infrastructure, say people in the know. It is located 60 km from Burgas, close to Tsarevo and Primorsko. The half-kilometer long beach is more than 40 m wide, covered with soft golden sand, and opposite Strandzha Mountain. A large part of the area next to Oasis is a nature reserve. Well organized place with a surf school, three beach bars, an outdoor swimming pool of Olympic size, a children's pool, many sports facilities. For the security of the owners and guests, round-the-clock security and access control is provided. A place for people with fat wallets and pets.

Rusalka

Rusalka (meaning Mermaid) is a fabulous seaside resort north of Cape Kaliakra. It is located 20 km east of Kavarna, 35 km from Balchik and 90 km from Varna.

It is located in the bird bay nature reserve, also known as Tauk liman and Nanevska tuzla.

Exotic with the incised rocky coast, small and cozy beaches, centuries-old oaks. Near the resort there are mineral springs with a temperature of 32 degrees. A rich archaeological reserve - the oldest monuments here are from 8,000 years ago. Rusalka has 500 double bungalows along the seashore. Here you can engage in a variety of sports - from tennis to archery to horse riding.

Riviera

Riviera - from a place of recreation for high-ranking party cadres from home and abroad before November 10, today Riviera has become a thriving luxury holiday village. It is located 17 km from Varna and has an area of 12 hectares. It has all the extras of an elite place - its advantages are that it is located in a park with centuries-old trees, on the very seashore, with its own beaches in sheltered coves. There is also a natural mineral spring. The famous rock monastery Aladzha Monastery is also nearby.

Dyuni (Dunes)

Dyuni beach is among the most luxurious on the Southern Black Sea coast. It is part of the holiday village of the same name, which is on the territory of a national nature reserve. It was built in socialist times. The project was realized in 1986, after the joint work of historians and architects. Completely renovated in 2000, the complex has preserved the coziness and romance of the Bulgarian past.

The Black Sea coast of Bulgaria is very suitable for observing interesting and rare species of birds. The reason for this is that the it passes over Via Pontica – one of the main migration routes of migratory birds from Europe to Africa. Numerous reserves, located along the entire coast, preserve rare and protected plant and animal species. A good attitude towards nature and its wealth rewards us with wonderful riverside forests, beautiful areas and rich biodiversity.

The Bulgarian Black Sea coast is rich with long golden beaches, clear sea and an incredible variety of resorts and holiday complexes. All guests find their paradise here - families with children, young people looking for fun, and nature lovers who prefer a quiet and peaceful vacation.

The lands along the Bulgarian Black Sea coast have been inhabited since ancient times, and today extremely valuable historical monuments can be seen in many of the seaside towns and resorts. This provides a wonderful opportunity to diversify the sea vacation and to touch the culture of bygone eras. Among the most interesting cultural sites is Old Nessebar - a cultural monument under the auspices of UNESCO.

The Bulgarian Black Sea coast offers numerous and varied opportunities for rest and entertainment. 378 km long, it includes 70 beaches, many bays, picturesque estuaries with beautiful longose forests and a wonderful combination of mountain and sea climate. Bulgarian beaches are popular all over the world for their fine and clean sand. In 2010, 11 Bulgarian beaches were awarded the Blue Flag - an assessment for a clean and ecological environment.

The Black Sea has low salinity and its tides are almost imperceptible, making it suitable for swimming in the summer months. Its temperature in summer is moderate – it rarely exceeds 28 ° C, being lower in the north and higher in the south.

The proximity of two mountains - Stara Planina in the middle of the Black Sea coast and Strandzha in the south - contributes to the pleasant and beneficial climate and is a great prerequisite for the combination of sea vacations with clean mountain air.

A walk in the Iskar gorge

The proverb that water finds its own way and, although it is the softest element, can break through stone, exquisitely describes the majestic beauty of the Iskar gorge. Cut deep into Stara Planina, the river glides, flexible and confident, from Novi Iskar, a town almost on the doorstep of Sofia, all the way to Mezdra and Karlukovo, and in its waters you can see white limestone rocks, wonderful waterfalls, caves and legendary monasteries. The landscape is a kind of art therapy for the eyes and the heart, because the hills and elevations are covered with lush greenery at the beginning of spring and retain their shady serenity until mid-autumn. They often compare the wonderful views along the Iskar gorge with Switzerland, but the rich history, natural contrasts and diversity of plant and animal species are unique.

It is an interesting fact that the gorge occupies a place in the heart of the patriarch of Bulgarian literature Ivan Vazov, the author of the Renaissance novel "Under the Yoke", who was impressed by the dignity and beauty of this place. The railway was laid in 1887, an event reflected in Vazov's classic story "Grandfather Yotso is Watching". Today, on the rocks opposite the railway line along the Iskar gorge, near the village of Ochin dol, stands the 5-meter tall figure of the strong old man who welcomes the freedom and progress of his homeland.

Whether you take the train ride, tour the area by car or join an adventure hiking group, Iskar Gorge will fill you with buzzing energy, joy and wonder. The area offers wonderful opportunities for authentic eco- tourism, healing air, clean food and direct contact with the history and literature of Bulgaria. Today, the Vazov hero embodied in stone reminds us that even when the eyes are blind, the heart sees and leads to the right path.

Probably the most remarkable destination is the village of Lakatnik (which is located 8 km from Lakatnik station, to which a modern tourist train will take you), about an hour's drive from Sofia. The locality is so named because of the resemblance to a bent elbow. Opposite the Lakatnik station is the Zhitolyub karst spring, formed by two underground rivers under the Temnata Dupka cave, at the foot of the Lakatnik rocks. Rock phenomena with a height of up to 250 m excite the imagination with their bizarre forms - towers, pyramids and natural obelisks, among which there are over a hundred caves and chasms. The deepest among them is the Dark Hole (9 km). Lakatnik rocks are very popular among climbers, with over 300 routes. You cannot miss the Alpine meadow and the red house of the Eagle's Nest shelter, built in 1938, nestled in the sheer cliffs.

The epic story of the origin of the village of Zverino tells of a brave hero who dared to settle in this wild place, inhabited only by wolves and beasts, together with his beautiful young wife. They called him Beast Neno, and he gave his name to the village. Nearby is the Cherepish Monastery of Assumption, built at the end of the Second Bulgarian Kingdom. Destroyed many times, the monastery was rebuilt to become a center of literature and enlightenment during the Renaissance. Brave spiritual awakeners such as Sophronius Vrachanski and revolutionaries found refuge here, and writers Ivan Vazov and Aleko Konstantinov found inspiration and rest.

Six kilometers from the town of Svoge, near the village of Tserovo, rises the rock formation Juglata (that is, the Camel), as if sculpted by the hands of a modernist sculptor, but actually a creation of time and nature from 250 million years ago.

Ten kilometers from Svoge is the village of Iskrets, where in 1908 King Ferdinand I donated the funds and issued a decree for the construction of a sanatorium for the treatment of tuberculosis, and the Holy Synod donated the lands. The place was chosen because of the microclimate of Iskrets, with crystal clear air, forests and river, minimal number of foggy days, ideal altitude and a park with 250 rare tree species. The view of opposite green hills and symmetrical circular meadows, the bleating of goats grazing in the valley and the song of birds at dawn add to the healing effect by harmonizing body and mind. In the courtyard of the sanatorium stands the Assumption Monastery, dating from the 13th century. In its current form, the beautifully painted church was built in 1602, and the heptagonal baptismal confessional is unique in Bulgaria and the Balkans.

In the village of Eliseyna, 30 km from Svoge in the direction of Mezdra, the Church of the Holy Prophet Eliseus and the Monastery of the Holy Mother of God, also known as the Seven Thrones, attract aesthetes and pilgrims. The clean mountain air, greenery and coolness during the summer months accentuate the laconic beauty of these places of faith. Legend has it that the monastery was founded by seven boyar brothers who came from Bessarabia in the 11th century. Historians confirm that the holy monastery was built during the period of the Second Bulgarian Kingdom. The monastery has its own library with old liturgical books, one of which was a gift from the Russian empress Catherine the Great.

20 flavors from Bulgaria - what, where and how

Rich, natural, fresh, rich and aromatic - this is the taste of Bulgaria. Thanks to the location and history of the country - the cradle of the Thracian wine culture in the center of the Balkans, on the threshold of the Orient and in the middle of the land kissed by all the goddesses of fertility, the Bulgarian culinary tradition combines the best of Slavic, Greek, Turkish cuisine and even the saddlebags of the ancient equestrian peoples of Central Asia. Many dishes, as their names suggest, are borrowed from Turkish Ottoman cuisine, which in turn draws inspiration from Greece, the Crimea and the Caucasus. The flattering rays of the sun, the crystal clear spring water, the proud power of the mountain and the mischievous sea winds give a special flavor that makes Bulgarian dishes unforgettable.

The twenty legendary flavors that we present here are conditionally divided into four categories - sea, mountain, merry table and sweet delights. Approach them with a healthy dose of imagination and experiment and combine with a brave heart - so far there is no known way to go wrong. It is even possible to create your own unique menu and bouquet of flavors to take with you and turn into an exotic addition to your usual table.

Cheers!

Black Sea delights

T**arator** - Addictively delicious cold yogurt soup, finely chopped cucumber, dill, crushed walnuts, crushed garlic and delicate pearls of sunflower oil or olive oil floated to the surface. A few years ago, a famous chef (master chef) turned the ovations of a world culinary competition, turning the tarator into a frozen appetizing sorbet. There is no better way to lighten up and cool down in the summer heat and midday haze at the seaside. A strong friendship connects the tarator with the next finalist in our ranking, namely mastic.

Mastica – a high-alcohol aniseed drink from the family of ouzo, perno and pastis, which is usually drunk very chilled ("in crystals") and with a few drops of water or ice, which turn it from transparent to a milky white fragrant liquid. The legendary sea cocktail "cloud" is obtained by adding a few sips of mint liqueur to the mastic, forming serene aromatic ambrosia that is capable of invigorating even the most sun- and seawater-sucked vacationer.

TARAMA CAVIAR – another faithful friend of the above combination. It is well beaten with oil, lemon juice, ethereal onion puree and fish roe in the middle of a slice of dry bread. An appetizing, unpretentious appetizer that cannot be compared to the aristocratic refinement of caviar, but it deserves to be tried.

BLACK SEA FISH - turbot, lefer, safrid, if possible caught before sunrise and prepared by the skilled hands of the local hostess. From Nessebar in the south, they serve the fish fried until golden or toasted on the grill with skordalia - a spicy garlic paste, or with a dressing of vinegar, garlic and devesil. The student version of these delicacies is the magical combination of "fried sprats and fries" - the tiniest, unashamedly grown-up Black Sea fish sold in the cheerful shoreside traps and paired with countless pints of draft beer.

Grape leaf sarmicki with yogurt - lean or with a little minced meat, the dish is found with certain variations in Greek, Turkish, Armenian, Jewish and Lebanese cuisines, but the key factor in the Bulgarian recipe is the size (as big as a child's thumb), the aromatic spices (fennel, parsley, chives and spring onions), the silky fine vine leaves from the asma in the hostess's yard and the dill and garlic yogurt sauce with which they are served.

Mountain flavors

With the full awareness that the culinary traditions of Pirin, the Rhodopes and Stara Planina (the Balkans) are quite different, we bet on the leading element and the desire for hearty, nutritious dishes that warm the bones of the frozen traveler and ignite his blood for new snowy adventures.

Bean salad - a typical winter, nutritious salad of ripe beans (preferably Smiljanski), chopped onions, roasted red peppers and homemade lutenica. Able to satiate starving vegetarians and whet the appetite of mountaineers.

Patatnik – a specific regional recipe from the Rhodopes, which is a patty with a local variety of potatoes, with a lot of butter, cheese and jodgen. Interestingly, the dish is not prepared in an oven, but on a sach – a round clay plate with a rim at the end, placed on the embers in the oven.

Lamb chomlek kebab - one of those tender and aromatic meat dishes that are prepared in a clay pot (pot, casserole or pitcher) and are a typical representative of the "slow food" movement, simmering for hours on low heat. Interchangeable with kaverma kebab or the famous Banska Kapama, which, in addition to three types of meat, also includes sausage or blood sausage, sauerkraut, red wine and aromatic herbs and spices.

Lamb cheverme - Bulgarians jokingly call the days around the feast of Saint George (May 6) "the silence of the lambs".

And they honor the patron saint of fighters, shepherds and shepherds with a freshly slaughtered whole animal - a lamb, a goat or a kid, which is roasted on a grill, in an oven or stewed in a dug pit. The cooking lasts at least 5-6 hours, until the meat is evenly baked to a golden crust, constantly basting it with its own fat, and in some regions with honey. The experience and taste of the meat is unforgettable under the shade of ancient trees and in combination with the intoxicating red wine.

Red wine - a stay in the lands of the Thracians, the most sophisticated wine culture of antiquity, would not be complete if you did not try at least a few types of wine from the unique local grape varieties. Trust your own intuition or the sommelier's advice and enjoy the divine properties of merlot, cabernet Sauvignon, Ruby, Mavrud, Pamid and Gamza.

Merry table

Shop salad - white and as if covered in snow on the outside, colorful and delicious on the inside, this salad has been around for decades as the culinary business card of Bulgaria. Its name suggests that it is typical of the region around Sofia, called shopluk. The authentic Shop salad includes roasted red peppers, finely chopped fresh onions, garden cucumbers and tomatoes, lots of parsley and a thick covering of grated white cheese as dense as the snow cover of Vitosha. Even if you fall in love with it, be sure to try its less famous, but equally delicious sisters - Dobrudzha, Ovarska, Kalugera and Snezhanka. Always an appetizer with the Bulgarian grape or plum brandy.

Wolf appetizer - behind this euphemism lies an unimaginable variety of cold meat appetizers - dried goat and beef pastrami, various sudzus and sausages, banski starets, venison fillet, sheep sazderma... Some of them are produced according to a traditional, kept secret recipe, others are typical for a given region and even a city (Ban old man is made only in Bansko, and Veliko Tarnovo, Gorna Oryahovitsa and Karlovo compete for the championship in making the tastiest sudjuci and lukanki).

Pogacha - puffy, fragile and irresistibly delicious bread, on which the skillful hands of the hostess sculpt fabulous scenes with birds, flowers and braids. In some regions, you will be served tutmanik or milinki instead of the bread. With them, every dish becomes tastier, and separately, served with cheese, merudia (colored salt) or honey for breakfast, they are able to keep you full all day.

Banitsa - another trademark of Bulgarian cuisine. It is truly lucky to taste an authentic grandmother's pie with crusts specially rolled out by some stooped old woman in the village, with eggs just laid by the chickens in the yard and a filling of white cheese, spinach or pumpkin. But given the circumstances - authentic Bulgarian grandmothers are becoming fewer and fewer - you can trust the works of good pastry chefs and bakeries.

Rakia - although they do not call their national alcoholic drink by such poetic names as water of life or fire water, Bulgarians are ready to suffer and rise in defense of this spiritualizing liquid. No amount of administrative regulations and regulations managed to eradicate the tradition of home brandy brewing, although the colorful copper cauldrons became invisible. Any self-respecting Bulgarian will pull out of the deep reserves a bottle of thick, amber hot brandy to stun a guest. Each region is proud of its unique drink - Trojan plum, Burgas grape, Silistren apricot and even Karlovy pink...

Sweet Temptations

Most traditional sweet delights are borrowed directly from Turkish cuisine - syrupy delights such as baklava, revane and tolumbicki, others are simple, but unattainably delicious desserts, and there are also such masterpieces that appeared unknown how, why and when in a single place in the country, becoming a legend for generations.

Sheep yogurt with a garnish of honey and walnuts, blueberry jam or green or ripe fig jam. Explanations are unnecessary here, the combination of the dense, perfectly balanced taste of the thick yogurt and the ethereal sweetness of the jam gives the perfect dessert after a hearty meal or as a light snack on hot summer days.

Katmi - thick, porous pancakes, which are prepared in a clay pot over an open fire and eaten abundantly garnished with blueberry jam, honey or liquid chocolate. A divine taste that is punished with thousands of calories.

Damgi – an apocryphal dessert that is made only in Sozopol, crispy lacy sweets in the shape of a wheel made of cheruk according to a recipe secretly brought from the court of the Byzantine Vasilevs, as the legend says.

White jam - another forgotten aromatic delight that is present in the childhood memories of most Bulgarians. There are at least three recipes for a thick sticky confection of this name, which is served scooped up with a spoon and dipped in a glass of water, a fixture at ladies' gatherings from the late 19th to mid-20th centuries. In the authentic version, the secret agent in the recipe is chuven root, but in its modern version, the white jam is made from glucose, sugar, egg whites, lemon juice and essence.

Baklava, tatlias and saralias – classic oriental pastries with walnut filling, richly soaked in sugar syrup. If you're watching your figure, it's best to replace them with fresh fruit from some grandfather's garden at the market - the sweet, cooling core of ripe watermelon, honeydew melon crescents, sticky-sweet figs, heady apricots and peaches will fill you up without guilt. And they will inspire you to enjoy life!

Culinary traditions of the Balkan

FROM A BIRD'S EYE VIEW, the Balkans resemble a giant who is tired of carving peaks and hiding untold treasures in the bowels of the earth and has laid down to take a momentary nap in eternity. Stara Planina stretches along Bulgaria and is steeped in the scents of centuries-old forests, wet grass, medicinal herbs, rivers with ice-cold water, miraculous springs, beautiful samovars and songs about brave voivodes and unyielding beauties.

Crafts, trade, creativity and cuisine flourished here for centuries. Each town is proud of preserved authentic recipes, subtleties and secret ingredients. The water is sparkling and ringing, the bread has a crispy golden crust, the milk is thick and delicious, and the pastry is thin and sweet. The culinary wealth of this region is a logical consequence of the moderate climate, the specific location, the proximity of the mountain and the character of the local people.

Trojan's Plum Elixir

Troyan arose in the 15th century as a roadside settlement at the beginning of the Troyan Pass and is named after the Slavic mountain god Troyan. A legendary specialty is the Trojan plum brandy, which has been prepared since the 14th century in the Troyan Monastery - a beautiful monastery located on the banks of the Cherni Osam River and famous for its incredible wood carvings and frescoes created by the greatest Renaissance artist, Zahari Zograf. The fame of the fiery elixir spread around the world in 1894, when Sliven brandy was presented at a competition in Belgium. More recently, Trojan plum ragweed has been recognized and licensed as a regional specialty in the EU and USA. The authentic recipe is shrouded in mystery, but some of the subtleties include well-ripened local prunes that are ground on the day of harvest, the addition of 40 Balkan grasses and herbs, and aging in small oak barrels. The flavor of the brandy unfolds when served with skewered Trojan bacon, White Man (sheep's yogurt, cheese and roasted red peppers), mouth-watering wedding wheat and roasted plum pestil with walnuts. The ideal time to visit Troyan and the village of Oreshak nestled under its wing to taste these delights is the National Exhibition of Arts and Crafts and Applied Arts (held from 1971 to the present) and the Festival of Plum and Plum Brandy (since 1992) in the month of September.

If you visit Troyan in winter, be sure to drop by Apriltsi, a town in the heart of the Central Balkans, nestled between the Severen Jendem nature reserve and the peaks of Triglav, Maragidik and Botev. Here in the month of February, a competition and tasting of mild heated brandy and dishes with bacon is held.

The song of the bread

Along with fire and water, bread is revered as a mysterious mediator between the worlds, a magical food that gives strength and courage. Bread, like local songs and legends, requires a particularly melancholic, almost mystical vocation. Balkanians believe that bread has a soul and say that kneading bread should be like swaddling a diaper and playing with a small child - gently, carefully, with love and immense patience. There is nothing more magical than a winter evening spent in the kitchen of a local housewife creating the miracle of bread. The fluffy dough rises shyly under snow-white messals to pass through the consecration of the fire in the oven and become a huge samoun with a golden, crispy crust and a porous, perfectly baked core. Eat a piece of warm bread with Teteven buttercup, gathered the sun and blue of the plants in the grandmother's garden and grilled red peppers, garlic, parsley and roasted tomato, and you will know the delight of Balkan cuisine - pure, essential and open.

Fish brine

Teteven is not the only place in Bulgaria where the famous river fish soup is prepared, but the local soup is famous thanks to its spicy taste and the recognition of the writer Nikolay Haitov, who mentions it as his favorite dish "both in this world and in the next". ". The unforgettable taste of the fish brine is due to the combination and quality of the ingredients - seven river fish, mainly barbel from the icy waters of the Cherni and Beli Vit rivers, two river crayfish, two perfectly ripe and grilled tomatoes, several hot peppers, garlic and generous a connection of herbs and grasses. The boiled soup is left to age for at least a few hours before serving. In the summer, it is even eaten cold, as an excellent appetizer for the local plum brandy.

The trademark of Elena Balkan

"**E**very master of venison leg and fillet has his secrets," assure the people of Elena. "However, the most important thing is that the pig must have been raised in the Elena Balkan, in the fresh air." The technology seems really simple – legs, shoulders and fillet are salted and left in a special barrel. The duration of this process varies – about two months for the legs and a maximum of ten days for the fillet. Then the salted meat is left to dry and mature in an airy place. Back in the day, the legs were hung to dry in special "cells" in the room where the home hearth was, so that it would smoke.

For several years, on the last Saturday of October, the city of Elena has become the epicenter of culinary events in the country. Tastings and awarding of the famous specialty are accompanied by a folklore program and abundantly washed down with deer plum brandy.

The history of the Balkan town of Elena is shrouded in romance. They say that a path wound through the beech forests along which a heavy wedding party was passing. The groom led the bride to his native village. Suddenly, robbers attacked the wedding party and kidnapped the bride. But she refused to marry the leader of the robbers, and he cut her down near the Konash bridge in the village that took the girl's name, Elena.

Sujuk has one name

The fame of veal sujucs, pastrami and sausages prepared in Gorna Oryahovitsa and Arbanasi dates back several centuries. In 1538, Sultan Süleyman I the Magnificent issued a firman, which, among other things, also concerned taxes from the production of sudjuki in this area. In 1861, the Gorno-Oryakhov sujuk was awarded a medal at the International Exhibition in the Italian city of Turin, and the Austro-Hungarian ethnologist and traveler Felix Kanitz mentioned the delicious specialty in his book "Danube Bulgaria and the Balkans" from 1882. In 2010, Gorno Oryakhov sudzhuk became the first protected Bulgarian culinary product with a certificate for a specific geographical indication in the European Union.

At the end of May, Sujuk Fest takes place in Gorna Oryahovitsa, where connoisseurs and lovers can try various homemade and company recipes and varieties.

Herbs and spices

Herbs and spices are the soul of Balkan cuisine and folklore. In times when there were few ways to preserve produce, spices and wild herbs were highly valued as a preservative, medicine and magical agent. In the courtyard of every Renaissance house, tender hands grew kitsch basil, which was associated with fertility and feminine beauty. Devesil is a favorite seasoning for river fish, jojen is the magic sprig that turns an ordinary bean soup into culinary poetry, parsley is present in all salads and summer dishes, without dill airy summer dishes lose their freshness and flavor, and indrishe gives that romantic charm to grandmothers sweets and jams, which helps us not to lose irretrievably the secret path to childhood.

"Why is soup the primordial and eternal companion of man? It is the joy of the poor to the poor and a means of relieving the conscience of the rich, accustomed to refined feasts and expensive pleasures. From all that has been said thus far, I suppose you have understood that about the creation of the world and in particular I know a lot about soup. But my knowledge in no way gives me the right to engage you with violent prose, so let's move on to something substantial and practical, namely: to cook soup."

Gabrovka wedge soup

Габровска клин-чорба

There are countless recipes for this "soup from nothing", whose name has become a household name in Bulgaria. The people of Gabrovo prepare it generously, with mushrooms, leeks, potatoes, rice and many spices, but they do not fail to tell the story about it, in which they laugh at human weaknesses with their famous sense of humor, but do not fail to end the story with kindness and a lesson.

... A merchant went around the villages to sell his goods. In the evening, he fell asleep in an unknown village and stopped at a grandmother's cottage to spend the night. He asked for something to eat.

"I'm poor, son, and there's nothing to eat at home…", replied the miserly old woman.

The merchant sensed what the matter was, but said nothing. He took a pan, filled it with water and hung it over the fire.

"Why are you heating water, son?" asked the grandmother curiously.

"I'm going to cook wedge soup," replied the merchant.

Oh, my, how do you make wedge soup?" What is this miracle?

"Give me a wedge, and I'll teach you how to boil it."

The grandmother brought a wedge from the donkey's old horseshoes, the merchant dropped it into the manger and said:

"Now, grandma, give me some rice!"

The old woman wanted very much to learn how to cook wedge soup, so she brought rice, then onion, and finally an egg. She gave them to the merchant, thinking: "Let me learn how to make klin-soup, then I won't spend my money to buy one another, and I will always eat wedge-soup!"

At that time the merchant tasted the soup with the spoon and said:

„Grandma, bring me a tiny bit of butter!"

The old woman also brought butter. After a while, the merchant asked again:

"Ya, grandma, bring another egg!" The grandmother also brought a second egg.

When the soup was well boiled, the merchant took the wedge out of the pot, threw it away, and sat down to eat.

The grandmother looked at him, looked at him, and finally said sullenly:

"Listen, young man, every old soul knows how to cook wedge soup!"

"Well, if you know, then why don't you cook it?" - the merchant laughed and continued to eat the delicious soup.

- Bulgarian folk tale

The rose in cooking and perfumery

From time immemorial and all over the world, the rose has been valued for the sweet, soothing effect of its fragrance and for the colors and shapes of its flowers. Its homeland is the Orient, but nowadays roses are grown in temperate climates all over the world. There are about 250 different species, including wild roses, not counting the thousands of hybrids. About 30 species of roses are described as odorata (fragrant), but only three of them, the oldest, are cultivated for their exceptional fragrance. These are *Rosa gallica*, the most fruitful, which originates from the Caucasus, although it is called French, Provençal or Anatolian rose. The second ancient rose is *R. centifolia*, which originated in Persia and is better known as the Persian or Isfahan rose. The third proto-rose is *Rosa damascena*, the damask rose, native to Syria. It is highly aromatic and is grown for its superior oil. The name rose comes from the Latin word *rosa*, which in turn is borrowed from Persian. The ancient Egyptians used roses in religious ceremonies, and images of roses have been found in the tombs of some pharaohs and their wives. Cleopatra had the floors of her palace covered with roses before she received Mark Antony and had her ship's sails impregnated with rose water when she set out on her fateful voyage to Rome. The Romans treated roses extravagantly - at feasts, slaves sprinkled guests with rose petals, decorated statues of the gods and adorned themselves with roses to protect themselves from drunkenness. Julius Caesar's gardens were famous for their lovely roses, and his gardener was among the most respected people in the city. Virgil relates that Aphrodite requested that Hector's body be embalmed with oil of roses. Gladiators believed that if they anointed their bodies with rose oil before a fight, it would make them invincible. The Hellenes also worshiped the rose, Homer sings of it in *the Iliad* and *the Odyssey*, and Sappho proclaims it the queen of flowers. A rose was depicted on the shields of Persian warriors, and the historian Ibn Khaldun testified that in the 9th century the province of Farnistan paid an annual tribute of 30,000 bottles of rose water to the treasury in Baghdad. Roses were brought to Europe in the 1st-2nd century, and in order to extinguish the pagan associations of the beautiful flower with the goddess of love Venus, the Catholic Church dedicated it to the Virgin Mary. During the Middle Ages, nuns and monks grew roses in monastery gardens and described their healing properties in priceless manuscripts. Even then, the rose was considered a mild laxative, sedative, antidepressant and aphrodisiac.

The spring rain did not make it colder;
the garden dawned and the nightingale embarrassed
whispered confidingly to the colorless rose:
"Beauty, finish the red wine!"

- Omar Khayyam, The Rubaiyat

The Roses of Kazanlak - the most recognizable business card of Bulgaria

In Bulgaria, the oil rose was brought by the Ottoman Turks in the 17th century, but it began to be grown industrially in 1894, when the first rose distilleries, which are open to visitors today, date from that time. The famous Kazanlak rose, grown in the Rose Valley, is cultivated here, where it finds the most suitable conditions for its development and produces the highest quality oil. It is used in aromatherapy, alternative medicine, cosmetics and perfumery. Some of the most famous, iconic perfumes in the world play on the theme of the Bulgarian rose and build their compositions on and around absolutes from the Rose Valley.

Today, Bulgaria produces 2/3 of the world's production of rose oil. A typical Rose Valley plantation has about a thousand rose bushes per acre, planted 90 cm apart in parallel rows. The rose plantations are replaced every ten watermelons and produce 2000 kg of flowers per season, from which only 400 grams of rose essential oil are obtained through steam distillation. In some years, the price of Bulgarian rose oil approaches the price of gold; a secondary product of the steam distillation process of oil extraction is rose water, which is particularly popular in cosmetics and confectionery.

The flowering period is in early May, when the plants are bursting with color and the air is filled with fragrance. In the dark of dawn, the pickers go to the plantations to collect the flower in large baskets, which are then taken to the rose room.

Rose Jam

Back in the day, housewives grew roses in their gardens to make homemade rose water to refresh the face and flavor cakes and chaises. In Karlovo and Kazanlak, they make a wonderful cherry pie with a pink color. The Rose Valley has given birth to such famous delicacies as rose jam, rose delight, rose tea, rose syrup, rose honey and candied rose petals, which are added to decorate cakes or to flavor champagne and white wine. Recently, candies flavored with essential oil of roses have appeared on the market, which simultaneously perfume, lighten and sweeten the life of the one who consumes them. Another local specialty is rose brandy, which, apart from its unique taste, has a proven healing effect.

LEGENDS OF ROSES

The Greeks say that it appeared thanks to Bacchus. At a certain feast he fell in love with a beautiful nymph and ran after her in the garden. She hung and tore her garment on some prickly bush, revealing her beauty even more. Out of admiration, Bacchus caused the bush to be covered with red fragrant flowers, as beautiful as the sides of the timid nymph.

According to another legend, Cupid bribed the god of silence with a rose to convince him not to reveal his affairs to his mother Venus. Since then, the rose has become a symbol of silence. The central ornament in the ceiling decoration is known as a rosette, which comes from the ancient custom of hanging a rose over the dining table to ensure that what was said at the table would be kept strictly secret (this explains the meaning of the Latin expression *sub rosa,* "spoken under a rose").

The legend surrounding the discovery of rose oil is also romantic and dates back to the Mughal dynasty. For the wedding of Princess Nur-Jihan and the ruler Jihangir, they decided to fill the canal that surrounded the gardens with rose water. The newlyweds were sailing in their wedding boat on the fragrant water and noticed that a greenish, highly aromatic oily substance was floating on the surface. It was a natural rose oil extracted under the influence of the sun's rays. Thus began the production of rose oil in India, Persia, and then in Turkey, Bulgaria and other parts of Europe.

Famous rose-scented perfumes

Many famous perfumes build their compositions on the Bulgarian rose, which salts, rounds out, ennobles and stabilizes the other aromatic notes. But there are also perfumes dedicated exclusively to the Bulgarian rose.

The magnificent perfume Very Irresistible (Givenchy) is dedicated to the magnificent harvest of the Kazanlak rose from 2005. To obtain 450 grams of absolute for this perfume, 450 kg of pink flowers were needed. The precious elixir is encased in an exquisite, rose-engraved bottle with the brand's stylish label. The perfume debuted in 2006.

The solifloral fragrance Bulgarian Rose of the niche brand Demeter Fragrance (2000) is an ode to the freshness and delicacy of the rose color.

Rose Splendid and Rose Absolue (Annick Goutal) are two cult niche perfumes. The first recreates the atmosphere of a rose garden after a spring rain - freshness, authenticity and incredible inspiration, and the second is an intense floral symphony of six types of roses, where the Bulgarian rose is the unsurpassed prima.

The perfume Highest Rose (Montale) from the limited Confidential Collection, made of the highest quality pink absolute. The creator of this masterpiece is Pierre Montal himself.

Other famous perfumes in which the Bulgarian rose is the main character are Allure Sensuelle (Chanel), Noa Fleur (Cacharel), Infusion de Rose (Prada), Sa majesty la rose and Rose de Nuit (Serge Lutens), Omnia Amethyst (Bvlgari), *Paris (Yves St Laurent)* and *Trésor (Lancôme).* The popular fashion brand Zara also did not remain indifferent to the Bulgarian rose and in 2012 launched the solifloral fragrance Bulgarian Rose. An even more original idea is the choice of a natural perfume from a small perfume workshop in Bulgaria, which will become a unique aromatic signature and a wonderful souvenir (Refan, Bulgarian Rose).

More valuable than gold

The ancient chroniclers described Bulgaria as a land of mysteries, golden treasures and precious raw materials. More than one Roman emperor came to heal his body and spirit in the thermal springs here. Everyone knows that Bulgarian rose oil is one of the classic masterpieces of perfumery. Famous world masters of haute cuisine rely on the aromatic, rare species of mushrooms for their creations. Aromatherapists from all over the world proudly state that they work with Bulgarian lavender. But that's not all... I invite you on a walk with elements of mystery and adventure among centuries-old forests and fragrant fields to discover the raw materials that entered the recipes of ancient magicians and modern masters of cooking, perfumery and synesthesia.

While the king feasts at the table,
my spikenard pours forth its scents.
My favorite is like a bunch of myrrh sleeping
between my breasts.
My favorite is like a bunch of henna fragrance
in the vineyards of Ein-Gèdi.
From Song of Solomon

Rose

According to some historians, the cultivation of the oil-yielding Kazanlak rose in Bulgaria should be attributed to the beginning of the 17th century, since in 1650 the rose water from Karlovo and Kazanlak was the main commercial product on the Edirne market, and in 1680 the first gulap was brought, that is, a pot for the double distillation of rose oil. But a careful reading of the ancient chronicles reveals that roses were brought to the Balkan Peninsula by the warriors of Alexander the Great after the campaign in Persia. From Pliny the Elder's Natural History we learn that the Thracian rose was one of the twelve varieties of the queen of flowers that existed at the time, and rose attar was one of the most valuable perfume ingredients, suggesting that already in the 5th century BC, roses were already grown on our lands. Moreover, the Valley of the Roses borders and even coincides with the Valley of the Thracian Kings, and the rose is a frequently depicted symbol on the walls of Thracian tombs, combining ritual and utilitarian purpose. This tradition has continued through the centuries, making the rose a national symbol and trademark of the country. Bulgarian rose oil was successful at the World Exhibitions in Chicago (1893), Liège (1905) and Milan (1906) to receive gold medals in Paris, London and Antwerp. Today, pink absolute, oil and atar from

Bulgaria are present in the arsenal of high-end perfumery, cosmetics, aromatherapy and alternative medicine, and in some years their price approaches that of gold.

Lavender

In mid-June, lavender fields in Bulgaria are covered in color and emit a joyous, mind-stimulating and heart-warming scent. The harvest hasn't started yet, so romantics can take a blue-purple stroll at sunset to soak up the subtle vibes of the plant prized by Greeks, Romans, knights and royalty. The essential oil of Bulgarian lavender is especially highly valued in aromatherapy because, thanks to the altitude and climate, it has a milder aroma and more delicate properties than the Mediterranean varieties.

Thyme

Thyme is one of the 400 medicinal herbs described by Hippocrates. The Romans cooked with thyme and drank a decoction of it at the end of feasts. Pliny the Elder recommends it as a cure for epilepsy and states that the patient should sleep on a bed covered with thyme to calm down and sleep, and recommends the potion against headaches. In addition to the cultivation of thyme for culinary, medicinal and cosmetic purposes, Bulgaria has a tradition of producing a special type of medicinal honey, obtained from bees that collected floral nectar from wild thyme.

Oak moss

The centuries-old oak forests of Bulgaria are the source of one of the most highly valued ingredients in perfumery - oakmoss. In fact, it is a type of lichen - a strange symbiosis between fungi and algae - that grows on the trunk and branches of certain types of deciduous and coniferous trees, with a color that, depending on the climate, season and humidity, varies from dark green through the root to white and shape, resembling deer antlers. The variety from the pine forests is especially highly valued by perfumers, as it has a specific aroma of frankincense resin, without which the most beautiful oriental aromas would be impossible. Bulgaria exports this valuable raw material to the perfume factories in Grasse, France, where it is distilled or extracted in the form of absolute and concrete, which in turn forms the basis of the famous chypre and fougere perfumes. The delicate, dry and changeable presence of oakmoss gives depth to aromas, ensures their durability and unlocks unsuspected metamorphoses in the general olfactory impression.

Saffron

In Bulgaria, autumn crocus has been growing for centuries, perhaps even millennia, since the time when the Greeks cultivated the plant and began to use it in medicine and cooking, but only in the last few years have successful steps been taken to grow the most valuable and expensive spice in the world. Just imagine – 150 flowers of saffron crocus produce one gram of spice...

Saffron first appears in an Assyrian botanical reference book from the 7th century BC, and its fame as a universal healer is astounding, as it is recommended for about 90 ailments. The word itself probably comes from Akkadian (the main language of Ancient Mesopotamia), but the leaders in the cultivation and trade of saffron were the Minoans. Frescoes from the Palace of Knossos on the island of Crete, dating from the Bronze Age, depict monkeys trained to gather crocus blossoms, under the watchful eye of a priestess or goddess. Another fresco in the palace depicts a woman applying saffron flowers to her punctured, bleeding leg, which no doubt speaks to the medicinal properties of the plant.

Tobacco

It is difficult to determine exactly when smoking and growing tobacco began in Bulgaria, as there are no reliable historical sources, but at the beginning of the 16th century, the tobacco plant was already brought and grown as a herb in our lands. Folk medicine recommended tobacco leaves for the treatment of wounds, scabies and other diseases of humans and livestock. A good guide is the fact that the first tax on tobacco in the Turkish Empire was imposed in 1687, with a decree ordering the collection of customs duties for exported tobacco through the ports of Vidin, Nikopol, Silistren and along the Black Sea coast. Production was relatively small. Tobacco of the Kabakulak, Staro seme and Rachkar varieties is grown in our country, mainly along the lower reaches of the Struma, Mesta and Maritsa rivers. In 1942, annual production already amounted to 65 million kilograms, and the value of exports constituted 40% of all exports, and Bulgaria established itself on world markets as a producer of high-quality oriental varieties.

Edible Mushrooms

Boletus, yellow and golden duck's foot, chanterelle, sheep's foot... These are just some of the wild mushrooms in the Rhodopes that are present on the menus of the most famous chefs in the world. Famous restaurants in Italy, France and Switzerland are supplied with porcini mushrooms - the universally recognized queen of mushrooms in our lands - precisely from the forests around Sarnitsa, Shiroka Laka, Smolyan and Chepelare. Forests, crystal clear air and abundant rainfall are the ingredients for a good harvest.

Silkworms

While kings and nobles in Europe relied on the trade caravans from the Middle East and China to supply themselves with beautiful silk, in Bulgaria spinning was a traditional craft as early as the 7th - 9th centuries. In the 20th century, the country ranked eighth in the world and first in Europe in raw cocoon production. Although strange at first glance, this is completely natural, considering the main requirement - presence of mulberry trees, which grow well in Bulgaria, do not require special care and live from 80 to 300 years.

Salt

S alt has always been a valuable commodity, thanks to its ability to flavor and preserve food and act as an antiseptic, but few know that the oldest saltworks, and perhaps even the oldest city in Europe, are located in Bulgaria. In 2005, during archaeological excavations of the Saltworks near Provadia, massive stone walls were discovered that defended the oldest known prehistoric city in Europe, which undoubtedly played an important role in the mining and trade of purified blocks of salt, which in ancient times performed the function of universal currency. The settlement has been dated to between 4700 and 4200 BC.

Divine flavors: the secret of monastery recipes

With your permission, I will hide the name of the monastery where I spent a blissful summer, the guest of the good abbot father... The wine... he cooled beforehand in the fountain, which sang sweetly under the shade of three old sad willows in the courtyard. At the little wooden table under the vine we spent the evening in quiet and inspired conversations about God, about the world, about the vanity of life and the mystery of death.

- Elin Pelin, Under the Monastery Vine

THE MISSION OF MONASTERIES in human culture is humble and noble – to shelter those who have chosen to devote their lives to worship. The beauty, grandeur and unique history of these monasteries, priceless shrines, chronicles and theological works attract countless visitors. As well as an interesting feature – almost everywhere in the world, the first documented cooking recipes were the work of the chronicler monks. The monastic notes later became cookbooks, medical reference books, and herbal books.

The Garden of the Virgin

The monastic republic on the northern Greek island of Athos, which arose in the 10th century, remains one of the most attractive symbols of Orthodox Christianity to this day. One mountain, twenty monasteries and twelve small monastic settlements (sketes) - the garden of the Virgin. The main element in monastic life is prayer. A large part of the monks' day is spent in the church, in services and prayers for all humanity, which last for several hours. Athos monasteries participate in various charity campaigns – they protect refugees, organize youth programs, help drug addicts. Yet the Holy Mountain stands apart from the rest of the world. Since the calendar here is based on the Julian calendar, Athos is 13 days behind Europe and the world. The monastic day begins at sunset, that is, about five hours before midnight. The menu of the monks is not discussed, but here everyone is long-lived and does not suffer from the diseases of the modern world. The secret - clean food, good wine, physical labor and mental harmony. The ancient Greeks called this type of nutrition *macrobiotics*, that is, *big life, long life* or *full life*.

Each monastery is completely self-sufficient from its own vegetable and fruit garden, vineyard, pasture and olive grove. Deliveries from the mainland are kept to a minimum. Most monasteries have a small harbor and fishing boats.

The monastic meal is a religious ritual that takes place twice a day - morning and evening. The monks eat in complete silence, reading the Holy Scriptures. The meal lasts about twenty minutes, the end is announced by the ringing of a bell. Menu and mode are unchanged. Monday, Wednesday and Friday are fasting days, without animal proteins, wine and vegetable oil. The dishes are boiled or steamed, but this does not limit the menu. The rest of the days are called modest and include fish, cheese, eggs, yogurt and red wine. Breaking the fast after fasting is a joyful event under the sign of culinary abundance: fish, baked goods and even sweets. Fasting and self-discipline are the essence of virtue, say the monks.

The Ambrosia of the Troyan Monastery

A stone's throw from the city of Troyan, tucked away in the picturesque village of Oreshak, the holy Assumption Monastery is shrouded in legends. Not only because of the miraculous guide icon Holy Mother of God Troeruchitsa. According to tradition, the original icon was brought by hermit monks from Athon in the early 17th century. The history of the monastery is connected with miracles, healings, attempts and rising from the ashes. Dozens of Renaissance figures studied here, the frescoes in the church are the work of the famous Bulgarian painter Zahari Zograf in the period 1847-48. And here the plum ambrosia of the Balkans is made - the famous Trojan plum brandy. The authentic recipe is shrouded in mystery, but some of the subtleties include well-ripened local prunes that are ground on the day of harvest, the addition of 40 Balkan grasses and herbs, and aging in small oak barrels. Troyan brandy has been around the world since 1894, when it won a bronze medal at a competition in Belgium, and today it is licensed as a regional specialty in the EU and USA.

The legendary specialties of the Trojan monks do not stop there. Humble in appearance, but irresistibly delicious is the fragrant bean soup, with black beans for the unforgivable sins and white beans for those that the mind cannot distinguish whether they are sin or not, as told in the wonderful story of the classic Elin Pelin. If you are lucky enough to visit the Troyan Monastery during fasting days, the meek monks will serve it to you with bacon on a spit passed through the purifying flame of the fire in the stone fireplace. And if they're lean... get ready for a sensory-explosive pickled chili.

I think and I do not know which is supreme in man — the soul or the body. Aren't they in fact inseparable, and doesn't the soul triumph over the joyful urges of the body?" — white grain.

- Elin Pelin, from the collection "Under the monastery vine"

10 dishes that a woman from Rhodope should know how to cook

We offer a ranking of the most popular dishes that are served on the Rhodope table and that are prepared with ease by a large part of the indigenous inhabitants of the Orpheus Mountain. These recipes have been preserved in the folk memory, passed down through the generations.

The phrase "The Balkans keeps its secrets" is popular. This is probably also the reason why the dishes in question are prepared differently in different parts of the mountain. A large part of the cooks, sharing the recipes of these authentic dishes, hide one of the ingredients that gives the specific taste. This is where the enigmatic nature of Rhodope dishes lies. But on the other hand, in this way, many variations are obtained that enrich the dish.

And in the end, the traditional Rhodope specialties are liked and preferred by both Rhodope residents and guests and tourists of the mountain.

Here is our ranking:

Nettle soup

This is the most prepared dish in the spring season. Whether it is cooked with potatoes or rice, the dish is extremely tasty, and because of the nettle ingredients, it is also very useful for the human body.

Keshkek

This is a very specific dish that is prepared with cracked wheat and beef. The result is impressive - it's like eating melted cheese. It is one of the most popular traditional specialties in the Smilian region and in the Rudozem villages of Vitina and Polyana. There is no season for this dish - it is prepared all year round, but it requires great skill on the part of the cook.

Sarmi

They are not only a Rhodope dish, but are one of the preferred foods in the mountains. With cabbage or vine leaves, they are extremely tasty and preferred by the people of Rhodope.

Kolaci, katmi, mekitzi

So many women from Rhodope are masters in preparing yet another temptation to which Rhodeopeans indulge. With homemade jam, yogurt or honey, these three foods are extremely tasty.

Smilian beans

The preparation of this dish also has a special technology in which the women of Rhodope are enlightened. And the spices that are added to the dish make it irresistible.

Tripe and trifles

During St. George's Day and Koch Bayram, and not only then, the male part of the Rhodope population likes to consume lamb trifles. Baked or boiled, their preparation requires a lot of time and great craftsmanship. One of the specialties is the stuffed tripe with rice, liver and vegetables. It's laborious, but the effort is worth it when you see the satisfied faces of men after consuming this cholesterol temptation.

Pita

Whether it will be wheat or corn, it becomes one of the mandatory components in the Rhodope table. But it is mainly the older women of Rhodope who are initiated into the secret of making fluffy pita. That's why everyone brags about loving mom's and grandma's cakes.

In the top 3 of the dishes, the preparation of which a woman from Rhodope should be able to prepare, we put:

Parenik

And here there are many options - with onions, eggs or meat. But the success of the dish is guaranteed only if the housewife witnessed how her grandmother or mother worked over the stove. At first glance, it looks like an elementary dish, but in the process of preparation it is found that this is not the case at all. Perfection is achieved only through experience.

Trahana

The true taste of this dish can only be obtained in the homes of the elderly Rhodope women, who over the years have mastered the successful way of preparing this culinary temptation. Maybe that's why everyone outside the Rhodopes longs for this dish and when they return from a long stay abroad (gurbet), or in the sessions when students go home to study, they order their grandmothers to cook them the delicious feast.

Patatnik

The laureate of Rhodope dishes. The rolled skins, the Rhodope potatoes and the intoxicating heat of the wood-burning stove on which the patatnik is prepared are loved by all Rhodopeans, and the combination of the dish with homemade yogurt brings bliss to everyone who touches this intoxicating atmosphere

TRAHANA HAS BEEN A traditional dish in the Rhodope Mountains for centuries. This feast has always been a main dish during Qurbani, weddings and other public events in the past. Today, this tradition is alive and it is also a main dish at various public events. Cooking also in a close family circle is rare because of the laboriousness during preparation. Therefore, cooking in a close family circle is quite rare.

The dish is prepared from products that are locally produced. This is the feast composed of what is born on the Rhodope fields.

Trahana is crushed dry corn, ripe beans, meat, butter, and animal fat, mainly sheep tallow, are added to it.

The preparation takes place in the following order: First, the crushed corn is thoroughly rinsed several times to remove the hard chaff, then it is soaked in water and heated to boiling. When the water boils, a thin layer of the remaining chaff forms on the surface, which is peeled off carefully, after which the ripe beans, meat, salt, oil and butter are poured. Intensive boiling begins for about an hour, after which more intense stirring is started in order to make the material inside boil equally and the temperature is the same throughout the vessel. Additional tallow, butter or oil is added to the cooking process, and since the cooking lasts a minimum of 4 hours, it is necessary to add boiling water. Towards the end of cooking, it is necessary to cook on low heat for at least an hour without adding a new amount of water. In some cases, the brewing can even last 6 to 8 hours. The old masters claim that the quality is improved by constant stirring and prolonged brewing.

Wait for it to cool slightly and pour it for consumption. Reheating the trahana is done carefully until it boils again, because there is a danger that the contents will turn sour.

Orphic Mysteries in Trigrad, Fire show for Orpheus and Eurydice in the Devil's Throat cave

The **Orphic mysteries in Trigrad** are one of the most interesting events in the summer in the Rhodopes. They are held on the last Saturday and Sunday of July. **The legend of Orpheus and his beloved Eurydice and the connection with the Devil's Throat cave** is beautifully recreated with **a fiery spectacle** that traces the legend from the moment of the wedding of Orpheus and Eurydice to the moment when Orpheus loses his beloved in the wilds of the Devil's Throat cave. It is believed that this was the beginning of this almost 3000-year-old custom, which we continue to this day!

The legend of Orpheus and Eurydice

Orpheus was the greatest musician and singer of his time, softening even the harsh gods of Olympus to the sound of his harp. According to legend, he was the son of the river god Eager, who was the ruler of Hemus (today's Stara Planina), and his mother was the muse of epic poetry - Calliope. She was also his teacher. Legends of Orpheus' talent were well known, as he participated in the Argonauts' campaign for the Golden Fleece. There, with his music, he drowned out even the songs of the magical sea sirens.

Orpheus fell in love with the beautiful nymph Eurydice, and their life together did not last long. Very soon after the wedding, Eurydice was bitten by a poisonous snake while she was picking medicinal herbs. The poison consumed the body of the gentle nymph and Hades took away the love of young Orpheus. For a long time, the singer was sad for his beloved, but the absence did not give him peace and he decided to look for her in the underground kingdom of Hades.

The young poet went to the sacred river Styx precisely through the Devil's Throat cave, through which he had to go to Hades and ask for his beloved back. Arriving at the river, Orpheus had to cross it, and Heron initially refused him. Then the talented musician played his beautiful melodies on his golden harp, and Heron was so enchanted by them that he took Orpheus across the river in his boat. In front of Hades and his wife Persephone, Orpheus sang again, and the song told about the passionate and beautiful love between him and Eurydice. The gods of the underworld were so impressed by the songs of the Thracian musician that they allowed Orpheus to take his beloved from the underworld, but on one condition. Orpheus was not supposed to look at his beloved until he came with her to the surface. So the two lovers set off again to their old life full of love, but at the sublime moment, just before they came out of the Devil's Throat cave, Orpheus couldn't wait and looked back to see if Eurydice was behind him. Thus he lost forever his beloved, who again returned to the land of shadows, and in the place a healing spring gushed forth. The Orphic Mysteries recreate the legend in the Devil's Throat Hall.

In the great hall of the cave The Devil's Throat, the entire legend of Orpheus and Eurydice will be recreated, marking one of the most beautiful and eternal love stories. The idea of the holiday is to take people back several millennia and recall the power of love. The Orphic Mysteries are a two-day celebration and are part of the Trigrad festivities. The organizers promise to recreate the great legend for us with a traditional Rhodope flavor. Many pipers and folk dancers will be present, the tourist association Orpheus promises. Visitors will enjoy a magical fire show, as well as kukeri and traditional Rhodope performers. The holiday will be memorable for every tourist who decides to visit it, as the event attracts more and more guests every year.

Don't miss out!

Visit the website below and you can sign up to receive emails whenever Mags Pie publishes a new book. There's no charge and no obligation.

https://books2read.com/r/B-A-KBUZ-DAGSC

BOOKS 2 READ

Connecting independent readers to independent writers.

Also by Mags Pie

Fin, the Explorer
Fin, the Fish of Syllable Sea

Standalone
All About Eggs
Dream Reader
With Knife & Fork Around the Globe
Чудесаторът
Love Spells
Любовные заклинания
Revolutionary Plates
Mystical Gypsy Magic
With Knife and Fork in Bulgaria

www.ingramcontent.com/pod-product-compliance
Lightning Source LLC
Chambersburg PA
CBHW072011150726
47999CB00002B/607